12 Steps to Better Mental Health

Be the best you can be

By Elizabeth Rose

Contents

Chapter 1

Get physically fit and eating well   p1

Chapter 2

Have a social network and build more friends, have a partner in your life   p3

Chapter 3

Bucket list and list of things you enjoy/ are fun   p5

Chapter 4

Try different tablets and find what one that works best for you   p8

Chapter 5

Sort out any debts and finances   p10

Chapter 6

Having goals   p12

Chapter 7

Stop trying to come off your tablets p14

Chapter 8

Having a career path   p16

Chapter 9

Build a safety box or tool kit   p18

Chapter 10

Recovering while in hospital & once discharged   p20

Chapter 11

CBT   p24

Chapter 12

EMDR p26

Chapter 1

Getting physically fit and eating well

Exercise and eating a healthy diet are both very beneficial to your mental health, increasing your overall health and sense of well-being. Exercise releases endorphins which are your brain's feel-good neurotransmitters, they can make you feel better and put you in a positive state of mind. Having a goal to work towards at the gym is a good idea and then you get a great sense of achievement when you reach your goal. Examples of goals would be to do the couch to 5K, to run a 10K, to run a half marathon or marathon or just to go to the gym twice a week doing weights and cardio machines or join a yoga class. The government recommends strengthening exercises like weights or carrying heavy shopping done twice a week and at least 150 minutes of moderate intensity activity or 75 minutes of vigorous activity or a mixture of both. Moderate exercise would be like walking at a moderate speed. Vigorous activity would be running, aerobics, tennis or swimming fast.

Exercise also can reduce your risk of heart disease, help your body manage blood sugar levels and insulin better, improve your mental health and mood, make your bones stronger, increase your energy levels and will also strengthen your heart and increase your lung capacity. Some particularly good reasons to get fit! Many antipsychotic medications greatly increase your chance of getting high blood sugar levels leading to diabetes and also greatly increase cholesterol levels leading to heart disease, so exercise helps to combat that. I know a lot of the medications for mental health can make you feel very tired, drowsy or sleep. It's a good idea to have a tea, coffee or cola before working out to give you some extra energy and so you can work harder and push yourself more.

Eating healthily is important too. I know some of the medications for mental health can make it very easy for you to put on weight. Some of you may be on strict lower-calorie diets. If so, it is even more essential that what you put in your body gives you all the vitamins and minerals your body needs. Unhealthy foods like cakes, chocolates, sweets, biscuits and pastries should only be eaten occasionally, perhaps once or twice a week. They are full of sugar and can lead to spots, lower energy levels, craving more sugary food afterwards and can lead to weight gain and blood sugar problems.

Healthy foods are brown bread, rice and pasta, beans, boiled potatoes, sweet potato, porridge, Weetabix, oat cakes, Ryvita, brown rice cakes, some dairy for calcium like yogurt, cheese and milk, eggs, red meat, chicken and fish and lots of fruit and vegetables. Home-made soup is excellent in the winter and lots of salads and fruit salads with yogurt are great in the summer. Fruit and vegetables fill you up lots due to their fibre and reduce cravings for more food afterwards. If you are vegetarian try to eat more foods with b12, iron, omega 3 and calcium in. The government recommends two portions of fish a week- one oily. Oily fish has been shown to reduce depression and help bipolar. It helps stabilize your mood and is an excellent brain food.

Chapter 2

<u>Have a social network and build more friends, have a partner in your life</u>

It's important for your mental health to be social and get out lots, meeting friends and family and being part of your community. It also helps to have a partner in your life. Everyone deserves a partner who can support and motivate them, be there as a shoulder to cry on at times and to share adventures with and prevent loneliness. You could meet a partner at work, at a local sports club, through a friend or on an online dating website which are a lot more popular nowadays. Having a partner can make you want to be the best that you can be and can bring out the best in you.

Friends and family are important too. Family could include your children, your parents, siblings and any extended family. Try to see your family regularly. They will be very close to you and know you well and can be there to support you at times of need and offer any help. They can be very caring and understanding. Don't be afraid to call them in times of need or ask for help.

Friends can include old school friends, colleagues at work, old colleagues from past jobs, travel buddies, church friends and more. If you don't have many friends because you have lost touch with a lot of old friends, try to make new friends and make more of an effort to meet up and stay in touch. Maybe you have social anxiety. It's still essential that you make an effort to have friends and go out. Friends can be a shoulder to cry on during tough times, someone to have fun and a few laughs with, to share good times together and create good memories. Good places to make friends are- at work, sports clubs, a walking club, church, volunteering, group travel holidays and charity treks. You could even go on Facebook and message a few old friends and see if you get some replies and re-connect again.

If you have bipolar, depression or something else don't be afraid to tell certain friends or family so they understand that sometimes you are not up to meeting and need to rest at home. You would be surprised at how understanding people are nowadays of someone with mental health issues.

Chapter 3

<u>**Bucket list and list of things you enjoy/ are fun**</u>

Sometimes people spend so much energy and time looking after their partner and kids that they forget the things that make them happy. Or maybe some people work long hours and work really hard but then have little time left to think about hobbies. It's important to make time for fun and hobbies and also to sit down at some point and make a bucket list. It could be 20 countries that you've always wanted to visit. I've always wanted to go to the Taj Mahal in India, see the beaches in Thailand, experience Dubai and Iceland and finally one day go to Paris for example. Other ideas are to write a book. They say everyone has one book in them. Also, may be doing a 5k or 10k, a half marathon or a marathon or maybe cycling if you prefer that. Charity treks are a really good idea where you might cycle across Jordan, cycle from London to Paris, trek the Amazon rainforest or walk the great wall of China. They would be memories to last a lifetime and well worth raising funds for charity and to do the trek. You may have other dreams like doing up a barn in France, saving a deposit for a second property to rent out, swimming with dolphins, riding an elephant or learning to play an instrument. Maybe you love sport and could learn a new sport or take it up as a hobby. YouTube do so many free fitness videos from yoga to core strength training or even better go out and meet new people and join a fitness club. You may also want to learn to cook and bake properly and could try to do 50-100 recipes! Try to think of as many things as possible for your bucket list.

Once you have a bucket list next is to list all the things you would like to do in your spare time, things you love and that make you happy. The usual things are going out for a meal with family or friends, going out for a few drinks, playing snooker or pool, bowling, going to the cinema or having afternoon tea. You may also really enjoy in the summer going to the beach, go carting, paintball, cycling along the coastal front, white water rafting, fruit picking at different farms, going to the circus, music events and concerts outside like Capital summertime ball or Reading festival, national parks, adventure golf, golf, rock climbing, BBQs and sunbathing, rope courses, tennis, visiting castles, picnics in the park, visiting nice gardens, going to a football match or even American football, drawing or painting.

In the winter you may enjoy a London bus tour, the science or history museum, seeing an art gallery, Winter wonderland, national parks, swimming with flumes, water inflatables with the kids, adventure golf October or April when it's not too cold, indoor rock climbing, swimming lanes at a large leisure centre pool, walking in different parks and ice skating.

Also think what activities you would love to do for your birthday or if you'd like to take a short holiday. LastMinute have great affordable days out and Virgin do brilliant experience days. Think of what events are on for each month of the year from New Year's Day parade, Chinese New Year in China Town, air shows, flower shows, the races- have a day out with live music, see Wimbledon, firework displays in November and New Year's Eve fireworks in London.

Next list where in the UK you would like to go for a short holiday. It could be a few days away camping or glamping- very affordable or staying in a caravan or hotel. Bath has hot springs, Cornwall has surfing, Scotland has the northern lights and Brighton has diverse shops for example. For hobbies make a list of all the sports clubs you would like to try from a local running or football club to tennis lessons and walking clubs or trying a local boot camp.

Lastly think what you could do while on your own when family and friends are busy or activities that are normally done on your own. Ideas are shopping, going to the gym, swimming, cooking, having a massage or a spa/ pamper day, doing a Park run, getting a takeaway, taking part in an assault course or colour run- (look online for local events) and playing an instrument or drawing/ painting.

Hopefully by now you've taken the time to think of all the things you enjoy or love doing. It feels good to put yourself first! When you feel like you need some more fun in your life, invite friends or family to join you in the activities you enjoy. Don't spend all your money on material things or always doing the same activities like eating out or going to the pub. Try something different for a change and create memories and see how much fun you can have!

Chapter 4

Try different tablets and find what one works best for you

For anxiety, depression, autism and personality disorders there are lots of different tablets to try. For bipolar, schizoaffective disorder and schizophrenia there are quite a number of different anti-psychotics. Some medications make you drowsy, really relaxed and sleep lots while others give you anxiety and insomnia. Some make you have uncontrollable body movements and others can give you bad constipation and a really dry mouth. Some are also well known for putting on a lot of weight so it's a good idea to monitor your weight for the first 3 months. Clozapine is an anti-psychotic which when taken you need to do blood tests every week for 6 months then every month for two years. You may need to try a few to see which one suits you best.

Everyone reacts differently to the medication. One person may have uncontrollable arm and leg movements while another person just gets a few minor side effects that are manageable. When trying a different tablet, you may want to slowly come off one and slowly go on another, so they overlap. If you suddenly come off one and go on another and you've been on your current medication for several years or more, you may get really bad side effects for a month or two. However you do it, persist with the program. It can take a good 2 or 3 months to settle on a new medication and for certain side effects to diminish.

You want to find a tablet which has minimal side effects that you can live with and where the medication is also very effective at helping you with your mental health. It's a good idea to use an app or journal to write a daily diary of any highs or lows, stress, anxiety, psychosis, number of hours of sleep and if you feel ok, happy or sad. Then later you can look back and report to the doctor how you have been and for how long.

Chapter 5

Sort out any debts and finances

If you don't work, it can be very hard to cope financially. It's good to have some spare savings of 3-24 months of expenses. This is helpful even if you have a job, in case you are made redundant or lose your job, in case something needs fixing in your house like you need a new boiler, laptop, washing machine etc or you have a problem with your car and need a new car. If you are working, you may also want to save for a deposit for your first mortgage. It can be hard to save. One method for saving would be for a whole year- don't have any holidays abroad, maybe try a cheap camping holiday in the summer, stop all take aways and eat out less. Ask your friends whether they can just meet for a coffee or a walk or play tennis if you have a membership. Maybe you have a gym/ leisure centre membership- you could ask friends to go swimming with you. You could also do less shopping and buy less presents and Christmas presents and explain you are on a tight budget. After one year see how much you have saved.

If you are in a lot of debt under £20K and have various loans and credit cards and are struggling to pay it all back, you could ask for help from a charity like Step Change. They will review your finances as to whether you could set up a small payment program or if you could even do a debt relief order (DRO) or a mini bankruptcy. With a DRO or mini bankruptcy your credit score will be greatly affected and not recover for 6 years, so you would find it impossible really to get a mortgage during this time. This is something to consider.

With a DRO you have one year to see if you can find a job if you are unemployed or to see if you could pay more towards your payments and if things don't change in a year, then all your debts are written off. Step Change is a charity that would arrange all this for you and speak to your creditors directly. You would no longer get letters requesting payments or any court orders. It takes a lot of the stress away regarding financial problems. You could also mention to them if you have mental health difficulties and they will work with you.

It is a good idea to get a mortgage as soon as possible as renting is like throwing money away whereas with a mortgage it is your own place. You could rent out a room to help pay the mortgage or share with a partner, friend or sibling if your salary is not high enough. You could also look at shared ownership as an easier way to get on the property ladder. There are some banks that offer mortgages with a 5% deposit for first – time buyers and government programs for saving for a deposit if you are 39 or younger with a lifetime ISA. The lifetime ISA is where you can save up to £4000 a year and the government will add 25%.

Chapter 6

<u>Having goals</u>

It's important to have goals to work towards in the next month, the next 6 months and the next year or two. When I was younger, I put so much effort into my kids and partner and making them happy that I forgot about myself and having goals. Having goals makes you feel you are striving to be better and makes you more determined and productive. It's good to write your goals down and try to read them every day.

Examples of goals might be to do with college, work- finding a permanent full time job instead of temporary and part time or reaching a certain salary, learning how to cook, reading a certain number of books, writing a book, finding a partner, getting married, living in the city or the countryside or by the coast and doing a parenting course if you have children.

Also, feeling stable on the correct dosage of your medication, trying different medications and finding the right one for you, sorting out your finances, doing family therapy, setting up a side business, doing therapy like CBT or EMDR, losing weight, aiming for a flat stomach, doing volunteer work, if your children do not live with you- aiming to see them more and have them sleepover, starting a fitness program like couch to 5K run or following yoga on YouTube or attending a class for a certain number of months, playing a sport well for a certain number of months, training for a half- marathon or marathon, going on holiday in the UK even for just a few days or go abroad, waking up earlier, having more friends, saving a certain amount of money and saving up for a deposit for a mortgage.

This is your wake-up call. You can think- I am going to sleep a few more hours, I am going to miss the gym and watch Netflix every evening, I don't have the energy for work, working makes me tired, the successful people are just lucky or have rich parents. Or think I am going to work really hard; I am ready to earn the life that I deserve, no more complaining, no more watching others succeed from the side lines. Today you have a choice, continue living a hard life or be successful in life. Choose your hard. Training lots at the gym is hard, being happy with an unfit body and overweight is hard, working on your marriage every day is hard, living in an unhappy marriage is hard, working in a demanding job is hard, living without a job and having hardly any money to spend and difficulties with finances is hard.

Start by doing one push up, start by reading one page, start by making one sale, start by attending one college class, start by writing one paragraph. Start today, repeat tomorrow.

Chapter 7

<u>Stop trying to come off your tablets</u>

This is a very important matter to discuss. It can be very tempting and often occurs where someone is so unhappy with the side effects of the medication that they decide to come off the tablets or they mess about with them, cutting them up or missing doses. This is very risky and irresponsible. You must discuss changes in medication with a GP or psychiatrist. They will know you well and hopefully have seen you before and can tell how you are doing and whether you are ready for a decrease in your medication or maybe you are struggling and actually need an increase.

Some people even think if they can manage without their tablets then maybe they would no longer have a mental health label, maybe they are fine, and the doctors are wrong. This is denial. You need to trust that the doctors know what they are talking about and have great experience and knowledge in mental health. It can take a full 3 months for medication to properly take effect or leave the body. Therefore, if you are reducing your tablet every 6 weeks, by 3 months or 6 months you could end up very ill. You really don't want to end up in hospital and have a breakdown or suffer severe psychosis if you are taking anti-psychotics. That is what can happen if you suddenly stop or start to cut up your tablets. Also, if you cut up tablets even with a pill cutter you can never really get exactly half or a quarter so all the time every day you are taking different amounts, and this could make you ill. It's best to work with your doctor.

Times when it might be a good idea to ask for a reduced amount might be if you are back at work and need more energy, if you have a new partner who is giving you good support, if you feel you are doing well and have no psychosis, hallucinations or paranoia or only a little anxiety and depression. Times to ask for an increase might be during lockdowns when social contact is limited and you are feeling low and isolated, if you are very stressed at work, if you have recently split with a partner, if you are feeling very depressed, suicidal, have psychosis or new hallucinations or paranoia. Also, after a big change or stressful event you might need to increase your tablets. For example, during court proceedings regarding whether you keep your children you might find extra anti-anxiety tablets help or an increase in your medication for 3 months.

Chapter 8

<u>Have a career path</u>

It's a good idea to try to go back to work when you feel ready, if you are not already at work. Volunteer work can be a step in the right direction and get you used to working again. You could also start with part time work or temporary/ contract placements. It's a good idea when you get a job to speak to your manager and let them know about any mental health issues. You may need to take more breaks or days off/ afternoons off sometimes. If you talk to a manager, they will understand better and be able to help.

Some good ideas if you get overwhelmed at work would be to call a partner, parent, friend or sibling for a quick chat. If you attend a community mental health service and have a care coordinator you could speak with them for some reassurance and emotional support. If you like shopping, you could go shopping in your lunch break or do a little online shopping to cheer yourself up. You could try taking some chocolates or sweets and a cola in your bag and keeping it spare in case you are having a bad day. You could also take a break- a coffee break and a toilet break, listen to some music, ask if you can go for a quick walk, go to a newsagents and treat yourself to some sweets or chocolates or if you are very stressed and overwhelmed and finding it hard to cope- take the afternoon off work. It is better to take an afternoon off rather than quit your job.

Also, take care if you become poorly like having the flu or covid and you continue to try to go to work. Or, if you have some kind of personal problem like a breakup with a partner or an issue with a family member. You need to remember at times like these to take it easy. You may not be able to get as much done at work and you may need to take some time off work to recover. It's better to listen to your body and take things easy rather than do too much and burn out.

It's really good to work and have a career path. Try to do something you are good at or something you enjoy. Work makes you feel productive and motivated. You are meeting others every day and out of the house which is good for your mental health. The money will also take the pressure off any financial worries, and you will have more money to treat yourself, go on holidays and to go out and do fun things.

Chapter 9

Build a safety box or tool kit

It's a good idea for when your mood may get very low or even suicidal or you are just very stressed -that you have a safety box, something that will help you in times of crisis. You can buy one from a department store- it may be called an apothecary box or a calming box. In it might be a headband, bath salts, a diffuser, pulse point oil, bath foam and a scented candle. You can put the pulse point on your wrists for a wonderful calming or uplifting fragrance. You can light the candle or open the diffuser for a wonderful smell in the room. Or if you are female you could put on the headband and have a soothing bath.

Another good idea is to make your own box. You can find lovely large colourful boxes at most card and gift shops. In it you could put some earphones as a reminder to listen to some music or write a list of music albums that are soothing or uplifting, some herbal tea sachets, maybe soup sachets for a hot cup of soup in the winter, a few wrapped chocolates, crisps or sweets, some cards and pictures from family, friends or children- whatever feels most important to you and will cheer you up. You can also get a few notelets and write on each. For instance, you could write- "type depression in the search engine on Instagram and it will give you some support". Or "watch inspirational quotes you have saved on Instagram". Try writing a letter to a parent, God, friend or just to no one and write to get all your thoughts out and de-stress and brainstorm solutions. You don't have to send the letter, you can delete it afterwards. Another note could say about calling a friend, family or Samaritans. Lastly what I find most helpful is a note that says, "go out"! You will feel much better afterwards. You could treat yourself to some chocolates or flowers or go shopping and treat yourself to something. Write some ideas down to give you that push you need to go out. Sometimes a change of scene, a treat and being around others lifts your mood.

Some people respond well to sensory touch and smell. So, you could include a small perfume or perfume sample, some hand cream and a face spritz. You could also include some photos to look at and print out some positive affirmations. You could write a list of all your happiest memories in life and print it out to look at in times of need. What works for a lot of people are- having a nap, some alcohol in the evening to unwind if stressed (but do not drink if you are depressed), go shopping, have a shower and moisturise afterwards, watch a film or have a herbal tea or visit a friend or family or spend time with your children.

Another good idea is to carry an emergency or crisis card in your wallet or purse. A crisis card can have on it a contact number for who to call in a crisis, a list of any helpful services like Oxleas and a list of a few things that may make you feel safe e.g. making sure you are not too hot or too cold, eat if hungry, lie down, call someone and music. An emergency card can include illnesses and mental health, allergies, date of birth, blood group and two emergency contacts. You can buy them from an online large marketplace.

Chapter 10

Recovering while in hospital and once discharged

If you end up in hospital it can feel like a scary place. Whether you have been very depressed and suicidal, had a breakdown with or without psychosis or some other major event where you need urgent medical care, it's a good idea to prepare for hospital by packing a bag, writing a list for future reference or letting a family member or carer know in advance of what you would need.

I advise packing the following- enough underwear, night wear and warm/ cool clothing to suit the weather including a raincoat. Check if there is heating or not in your room, toiletries, sanitary products if necessary, spare snacks should you not like some of the meals, spare water, a plastic cup and herbal tea if they don't have an open kitchen facility- a warm drink on a cold night works wonders, a yoga mat if you enjoy exercise as something to do, roll on deodorant as sprays are not allowed, moisturiser for hands. Body moisturiser can be very relaxing for women to use, hairbands, trainers and gym wear for the gym, an iPod is a good idea if mobile phones are restricted- listening to music can be very calming or uplifting. It's often a good idea to keep your phone at home or with a loved one or carer as if you are suffering from psychosis or had a breakdown, you don't want to be texting inappropriate messages or messages that make no sense, and you may end up losing friends because of it. Also, it's good to pack a small bag to put a mobile (when ready to have one) and money in when going out and to carry around the building- patients can be clumsy and easily drop a phone. Extra teabags- sometimes the medication makes you so drowsy that you need a bit of caffeine to wake up especially before meetings with doctors and nurses, slippers and trainers- trainers are the best shoes to wear as patients can sweat a lot and move a lot when in a hyper state and you can walk quite clumsily and easily fall over.

A pad and pen to write notes is helpful if mobile phones aren't allowed or your mobile battery has gone (it can be a good idea to write down or ask a staff member to help you write down meal times so you know when is a good time to go out, visiting times, phone charging times etc. A hairdryer for women (to be kept in the office as it has a long cable)- needed so as not to freeze with wet hair in cooler weather, nail scissors- especially needed after three or four weeks and can be kept in the locker if considered safe. Lastly for women- women can feel very self-conscious when they are not able to groom themselves as they normally do. Tweezers are essential after a few weeks and maybe a razor. Both can be kept in a locker and even make up could be added to the list as it helps women keep their confidence when around others.

Maybe you would even like to bring a pack of cards, colouring books, pens and paper to do artwork and books to read as you can end up with a lot of spare time on your hands. Lastly, perhaps bring your favourite jumper, blanket and snacks.

When in hospital you want to make the best use of your time there. Try to wake early so you don't miss breakfast and morning ward meetings with staff and other patients. Find out what daily activities they have or whether you can go to a gym. At first you may not be in the best state to have even accompanied leave or to do any activities but as you get better you can slowly do more things. After accompanied leave is going well you will get more time during the day to go out and later it will lead to unaccompanied leave if you are doing well. Try to use all your leave allowance and go out for a drink or snacks and a long walk. As you get better you can even ask loved ones, a partner or friends to meet with you and visit on the ward or ask if you can see them and go out together for a set amount of time.

Things do get easier as you get used to your surroundings, the medication kicks in (especially if your previous medication wasn't working or you weren't taking it as prescribed or stopped taking it), you get used to the staff and are more familiar with the other patients. You may even make some new friends. There will be lots of games on the ward like snooker, table tennis, chess and board games. You can have fun with other patients.

It also gets easier once you are allowed out more. As you get better and have unaccompanied leave you could even go on a bus or train and go back to your house and read mail, watch TV, sunbathe in the garden, do some spring cleaning or just relax. After going home for a week or two, normally soon after that you are discharged.

Once discharged home help may organise some groups for you to gently adjust back into the community. Groups usually on offer are things like cookery classes or pottery which can go on for 6-8 weeks. You may see a care coordinator from Oxleas every week as well and even a home help nurse to check in on you every few days to make sure you are taking your medication as prescribed.

To avoid ending up in hospital try to have a close family member or partner or someone who has regular contact with you to check in on you regularly. It's easier to assess whether your mental health has deteriorated if you are seen regularly and in person is best to assess how you are. Be upfront and honest and say if you have any low mood or suicidal thoughts. You can also say whether you have any paranoid or delusional thoughts, hallucinations or hearing any voices.

I have learned from myself and close friends with the same or similar diagnoses that we like to show our best side and believe we are doing fine and well even when we are not. We may just tell others we are stressed or having a bad day when we need urgent attention and our medication increased. It's therefore a good idea to take extra care right after a stressful event. Losing a partner, a job, new financial worries, any court cases, experiencing any loss, a new stress like this Covid pandemic- these events often mean medication needs to be increased and as soon as possible. Any mentioning of feeling suicidal needs to be repeated back to a doctor or nurse. It is likely medication needs to be reviewed and if the symptoms persist perhaps a different medication would suit better.

Chapter 11

<u>CBT</u>

CBT stands for cognitive behavioural therapy. It focuses on how your thoughts, beliefs and attitudes affect your feelings and actions. It's helpful for people with a low mood or depression, anxiety, anger issues, low self-esteem, phobias and severe stress. It is less intense than EMDR and similar in stress levels to counselling. You may have a session every week or two and may need to go for 3 months up to one year.

One good example of how CBT can help is practising thinking for and against a thought. For instance, a friend could be late for a lunch meeting. You may think the worst and think he has been in a crash or something bad may have happened. CBT teaches you to evaluate this type of thinking as to the reasons for and against this thought. When thinking clearer you may tell yourself that actually the traffic is really bad due to a local football match, and he had just come out of a meeting so he may be running late.

Other good techniques used are evaluating and trying to reduce thinking errors. Thinking errors can be black and white thinking, overgeneralizing, minimizing and maximizing, discounting the positive and more. By reviewing our style of thinking and realising how it is not helpful we can start to change it. We all interpret events differently and it's a good idea to try to tackle some of these unhelpful interpretations.

Other behavioural experiments are using surveys. By surveying like-minded people e.g., other parents if you are a parent or other friends you can see if they react to different events in the same way you do. E.g., for anxiety you could ask a friend- "how often do you feel anxious and how intense is it?", "what situations make you anxious" and "how do you manage your anxiety". You could ask 10 friends and then compare with your own answers and see how different they are. This gives you good insight into how bad your anxiety levels really are and whether things need changing.

Another good technique is trying behavioural experiments. For instance, you could feel like you can't face the world and get out of bed. You could stay in bed for a whole day or half a day and rate your mood and what you did that day. Then force yourself to get dressed and showered and stay out of bed all day and rate your mood again and list your activities that day. Is the outcome as you would have predicted?

Weighing up evidence for and against negative automatic thoughts can also be very helpful. Gradual exposure to fears can tackle phobias. There are lots of techniques in the CBT toolkit, I hope you give it a try and see the improvements in your mental health.

Chapter 12

<u>EMDR</u>

EMDR is Eye Movement Desensitisation and Reprocessing. A family psychologist in 2019 stated that EMDR can completely cure schizophrenia or schizoaffective disorder. It also helps people suffering from anxiety, panic attacks, PTSD or trauma. She said how doctors in Sweden had used it to cure others. It is like the new CBT. It helps you to become better at coming to terms with trauma that has happened in the past. It heals past trauma by re-processing past upsetting memories. Sessions needed can range from 4 to 24. It is quite intense so it can be helpful to do some counselling or CBT beforehand.

During the sessions you can get very emotional, cry lots and even feel panicky, stressed or very anxious as you re-live the upsetting memories. The psychologist will be keeping a close eye on you to know when to end the session or take a break and how to end the session with a nice relaxation visualisation. During each session you go back to an upsetting event and process the memories by re-living them and seeing where your mind takes you. As you remember the upsetting memories you may hug yourself and tap your arm or look left and right at the psychologist's hand moving or another similar technique and this helps to bring you back to the present.

It is like there was a block in your mind where you couldn't process the emotions in the past as you were too upset and now you are finally feeling the emotion and processing it, so it no longer keeps popping up as flashbacks or nightmares. It should help to reduce flashbacks and nightmares, but they may not go away completely. After you have felt the emotion and brought yourself back to the present with tapping or eye movements, then the psychologist may ask you to rate how upsetting the memory is. Hopefully it should be less upsetting and then you can imagine the memory, and everything going well, and play out a different scenario in your head. In this way you reprocess the memories, so they are no longer traumatic or upsetting.

It's a good idea to monitor your flashbacks and see when they occur. There may be a pattern for instance an ex-soldier with PTSD may remember war zones after hearing a loud bang, or someone who has trauma from being in hospital may take a bus which stops at the hospital, and this triggers a flashback. Try to write down when they happen, what you are doing and how you are feeling when they happen. This will be helpful information for the psychologist when doing EMDR.

Final Thoughts

Whatever your mental health, if you can engage with Oxleas or GPs, take your medication as prescribed and work well with other therapies like counselling, CBT, EMDR, employment support, peer support clubs or family therapy, there is a bright outlook for the future. I have known some with mental health who want to shout it out to the world and educate people on it and others shy away, reluctant to even tell many of their friends or boss at work. Whatever the case may be, I've realised it's important to look after yourself, do the things that make you happy and help you lead a normal independent life. And don't be afraid of telling others- managers, friends and especially family. People are a lot more understanding of mental health now than 20 or 30 years ago. Make time for friends and fun and remember how special, unique and worthy you are. Thank you for reading and I hope this book has been a useful insight into mental health and the 12 steps for better mental health.